FINISHING LINE PRESS

www.finishinglinepress.com

AN EVERYDAY THING

poems by

Nancy Richardson

Finishing Line Press
Georgetown, Kentucky

AN EVERYDAY THING

ACKNOWLEDGMENTS

Poems in this manuscript have appeared in the following books and journals.

Dogwood: "In the Cardiologist's Office"

Mobius: "Kent State Trial, 1975"

Plainsongs: "Transaction"

Calyx: "Myopia"

Teaching the Art of Poetry: "An Everyday Thing"

Voices of the Frost Place II: Youngstown, Ohio 1952

The following poems have appeared in the chapbook, Unwelcomed Guest, published by
the Main Street Rag Publishing Company 2013: *In the Cardiologist's Office, Myopia, On
the Street Where You Live, Kent State Trial, Fathers, Coyote, Undercover Dates, Youngstown,
Ohio 1952, In the Lab, Locusts, An Everyday Thing, My Mother's Hunger, Floater, Portland
1991, Transaction , Shredding, Under the Trellis, and Mayflies.*

The chapbook, *The Fire's Edge* by Finishing Line Press contains the following poems:
*Randomness, Fainting, Shale Play, High School Reunion, Fear, Returning to Kent State,
On the Street, Patience, Kent State Trial, Door to Door, Cake in His Head, The Fire's Edge,
Clarence and Anita, Spinning, Lines, The Blue Trail, The Accident, Listening, Untying, Pay
Dirt, Lost, Cake in his Head, Undercover Dates, Volunteers, The Paralegal, Fathers, Say, In
the Cardiologist's Office, Mayflies, and Later.*

Publisher: Leah Maines
Editor: Christen Kincaid
Cover Art: John Anderson
Author Photo: Judy Brook
Cover Design: Elizabeth Maines McCleavy

Printed in the USA on acid-free paper.
Order online: www.finishinglinepress.com
also available on amazon.com

Author inquiries and mail orders:
Finishing Line Press
P. O. Box 1626
Georgetown, Kentucky 40324
U. S. A.

Table of Contents

Notes

For Galen

The Fire's Edge

Randomness

Kent State, 1970

She slid from her bed on the morning of May 4,
chose the bright red blouse for the occasion
of the day of her death. Sometimes I wonder
how my death will come specifically the *like*,
the *what*, the *how*. Will it be after dinner I rise
from the table, grab the hot wire of an infarct
across my chest, or after the tenth visit
to the cancer clinic where the vile brew delivered
through the pic-line turns my skin yellow, then blue,
then white. But getting back to her as she slammed
the screen door, smelled the newly cut grass,
walked looking up at the pillowed clouds and
the man pointing the gun four hundred feet away
saw something extraordinary through his sight.
A dazzling red and gold flash moving in the parking lot.
A small sun come to the tarred surface. I rise
from my bed and offer to the gods of randomness
maybe, perhaps, if: life as hypothetical.

Kent State Trial, 1975

"The photos speak for themselves," said the Judge
to the students' lawyers. The jury puzzled over them,
but the photos lost their nerve. In this one the Governor
would shout, "worse than the brownshirts
and the communists, night riders and the vigilantes."
Or another, blue sky, clouds, a clot of guardsmen
huddled in the field, perhaps a picnic on a spring day
in May. If the photo had bothered to listen it might
have overheard their plans to turn in unison and fire.
But it was busy and they were whispering. Here now
tongues should be wagging, "the guardsmen turn
and level their weapons," and "the guardsmen shoot.
All together now, Fire!" But the words were prisoners
in their cells, banging their tin cups against the metal bars.
The photos went on in silence in cardboard boxes
in wet basements. The photos held their tongues.

Myopia

Who could live with a person who sells
vacuum cleaners to old ladies, sweeps
the dead skin from their mattresses
promising them a cleaner life?
All I felt was the heat on his skin.
Later in the dark, when the baby's cries
were like spikes in the mattress and
he wouldn't get up, I wanted to throw
his body off the bed. Words float away
like dust motes leaving nothing
but quiet air, the way the small silences
around a conversation alter the direction
of a thought and are seen, like dams
in a river, by the way the talk flows up,
over and around. I sat in front of the TV
serving the babies chunky food from jars,
the day Robert Kennedy was shot.
Sobbed for his lifted head, his empty eyes,
my silent life, and left then, along with
the unused words, drove down the
two lane road in my rusty Volkswagon
with the kids, headed for words like
insight, foresight, some other life.

Shale Play

In the Hampton Inn beside the skeleton
of the steel mills, men in T-shirts drink
their coffee before injecting chemicals
ten thousand feet below the ground,
fracturing the gray shale. In the lobby
dining space yogurt cups sweat in ice
and scrambled eggs quiver in the metal pan.
The parking lot is full. A billionaire plans
to develop Mars—*terrafirm lanscapes,*
pink hotels, iron-oxide sunsets. Red planet
evacuation site. Here in the Ohio motel
where the breakfast mess is being cleaned up,
the men have left to pump black ooze.
Trickling in after five they'll wash the guar,
benzene, from their boots—amble to the bar.

Patience

The voting machines of Ohio.

The poor breathe the quiet air
of corruption in the gymnasium
where the voting machines sit,
stout, winking hulks. The screens
dissolve in a storm of snow.
Votes float into errant flying digits.
Patience festers at the edge of the freeway.
Resignation waits in long lines.
The power brokers ride cheap tricks.

Returning to Kent State

In its countless alveoli space contains compressed time.
That is what space is for. —Gaston Bachelard

In the grassy courtyard of
the married student housing,
Derek and the Dominoes blasts
in blue moonlight, *Layla you've got me*
on my knees. Just up the hill
voices from the Tri-Towers dorm
float downwind, *can't stand it.*
Feel the bullet holes in the brick
as we pass by. On the hill
the metal sculpture, another bullet hole,
small tunnel on the way to flesh.
Pause and turn to see the scattered
bodies in still poses, in memory
lying in the grassy meadow.
Daniel Berrigan marching, just
out of jail his hair flecked gray.
The scent of candle wax, low voices
murmuring. Bill Schroeder's parents
standing in his spot in the shadow
of a tree, candlelight casting
shadows on their strained pale faces.

Undercover Letter Dates

At Kent State 1972

The writer had long talks with Jann Wenner
on the phone. Wrote a profile of Nelson Algren
for Rolling Stone. Said his father was a magician
who locked the pigeons and rabbits in a room
and went away. Strange noises and feathers
followed. One day I passed a desk in Taylor Hall,
his name carved in the wood: N. A. R. C.

Another said he was an education student.
Wanted to do a project with me. Take me
to a meeting in D.C. His tailpipe fell off
as we drove down Pennsylvania Avenue,
loud noises and sparks flying. In the index
of Michener's book his name and N. S .A.

Bounced

Kerry Campaign, Ohio 2004

We couldn't canvas without lit. And then we ran out of chum, you know, buttons and bumper stickers. Then the rolling bosses thing happened. The power washer from Iowa was replaced by the coke addict from D.C. with the black fingernails and the bad temper. The last time I saw her she was standing by a dumpster smoking a cigarette. The Voter Protection people came and put on a "training." They divided us into smaller and smaller groups. To groups of one. Busloads of travelers arrived, wanting Starbucks and chicken Caesar salads. A woman from Oregon called to say she would pay for meals with her credit card. We ordered the food and ate it. The card bounced. That's what you can say about it.
The whole thing bounced.

Fainting

I fainted idiopathically, which means
the cause was not apparent. Heart
accelerated, free agent of pace and rhythm
beating against my chest wall, room tilting,
legs soft, noodling. Then adult faces
hovering, small helicopters of concern.
I remembered only the sound of falling
cutlery, a band playing, voices calling
from far, far away. But those lost
unconscious moments exist somewhere
in the cosmos, owed to me by the fact
I have not lived them. *This is the time
for sleep* says the insomnia tape, *the time
to release your thoughts. You can find
them again but for now let them just slide
over the horizon.* You will find them again,
those unthought thoughts, unlived moments.
Out there waiting just over the horizon
where the insomniacs, the lost, the unconscious
have left them. Before their bodies gave up
their minds. Before they entered the deep,
dark and peaceful place and let them go.

High School Reunion

I open the Holiday Inn event room door to bodies
in advanced stages of jowls, paunches clutching
one another, grateful to have escaped the departed
on page one of the program. The preacher
in the purple silk suit and top hat thanks God for
the entire history between then and now.
Elvis's bodyguard's ex-wife flashes her
21-carat diamond ring at the gifted, who are talking
achievement and other theories of success, while
the abused classmate's husband stares fists at me.
The palm reader with the long brown hair and
lipsticked smile says, " I have had a fascinating life."

Fear

Kent State gymnasium, 1970

The air is thick with strobe lights and sweat.
On stage Jefferson Airplane sings for the four dead

and the nine wounded. Gracie Slick in a voice
like a dirt road, *we are outlaws in the eyes of America*

tear down the walls. Behind her on the screen
Jeffrey Miller's body leaking down the concrete

in blue staccato lights. Somewhere a door lets in a gust
of fear. *Tear down the walls won't you try?*

But trying's getting ready to run in fear's leather boots.
I scream, punching the blue mist.

Youngstown, Ohio 1952

I climbed the hill on my green Schwinn
at dusk when the air lifted enough
for me to see the fevered orange flush
of the open hearth on the horizon.
Tomorrow, it would rain ashes
on our '52 Chevy. Later on a field trip
to the mill I walked on a catwalk
above the mouth. The runoff turned
into the sour taste of ash on my tongue.
The men were so close their sweat
turned to powder on their faces.
The cast heat rose and billowed
my skirt into a small suspended
parachute. Later, floating in the haze
that wanting makes, I lifted off
beyond the yard, beyond the gray sun
imagining a clear trajectory.

In the Lab

The amputated frog's leg had jumped
when he touched an electrode to it,
wire sparking, the small webbed foot

clenching upwards in a myoclonic spasm,
so when he heard the thud of lead
on dirt, took cover, felt the white hot

pain along his spine, he wanted
to live life backwards, turn and run
up the hill between the dorms,

pull back the stone he'd let loose
at the jeep with the guardsmen
and the blaring bullhorn. Last night

he climbed into his bunk, his sheets
still warm, not waking to the black
helicopters, veering, slanted overhead,

their lights searching the bushes for
his shadow on Main Street. It is
yesterday and he slides into his Ford,

May wind on his face,
heads home to his shingled house,
bounds up the stairs to his room,

the muscles in his legs unclenching,
thinking of his last race, how he
had crouched over the track,

feet in place, breath held, ready
for the crack of the starting gun.

On the Street Where You Live

The squat and menacing man
behind the chain link fence
with the slicked hair
and a ten dollar bill says,
"here kids, go and get
some ice cream," in a tone
that means *ya gotta go and now.*
In the background Vic Damone
croons, *I don't care if I can be
here on the street where you live*
to the Mafia Don's daughter
with whom his engagement
lasts two months. *Enchantment
pours out of every door.*
Guests mingle. This is 1948,
twelve years before the bombings,
before Bobby Kennedy calls it
Murder Town. Before the poor man's
urban renewal. Before arson.

Volunteers of America

We are here to save democracy
where the clouds are soot
where street money flows
and the ceiling leaks toilet water.
Workers are gathered
with their earnest faces.
We say some doors
are too dangerous to knock on
even in daylight.
Take off your jewelry

Locusts

One hot July night when I was ten,

when my grandfather walked me around the park,
when hot misty air hung in the shadows under the street lights,

we came upon a tree blanketed in seventeen year locusts,
great brown piles of them
some crawling out of their shells
moving over others in a slow death dance.

What did I know of death?

That it might look like this,
crawling creatures, empty shells
waiting to be stepped on,
ground into fine brown powder,
blown away with the wind.

His heart failing,
what did he see that night?
Not death, but perhaps, the way things fall away,
transform; shell to dust, skin to air, breath to stars.

An Everyday Thing

Notes of the students' lawyers, Kent State Trial

one round was fired on the hill.

what did they say?

you can see smoke in the pictures.

good hair, the jury likes him.

find the impeaching part.

cause she's so pretty.

watch out for hearsay and conclusions.

did you see anyone carry any bodies?

he put the blame on me for his fuck-up.

you have any phenobarbital?

he gave the order to kneel and take aim.

if he hadn't heard the order to fire.

he's getting scattered, tell him to sit down.

can you help me cash my paycheck?

one person in troop G emptied their whole clip.

he's been ineffective lately.

the net gain is clearly worth the cost.

he had his hand on his holster.

Bill was not dead there.

I yawn to mask my true sentiments.

when you play in the mud you get dirty.

say thanks to Charlie.

isn't death an everyday thing for everyone?

he said if they rush us shoot them.

how come you're saving all the notes?

Door to Door

Let these people
not be home

let the flyers
blow away quietly

stick to the
chain link fences

let me not walk up
these concrete steps
one more time

stand on this torn
green outdoor rug

read the Persuasion Script
promise life

will get better
perhaps not now

perhaps in some
other person's lifetime.

Floater

Somewhere between a shimmy and a glide
the motorcycle wheels reach for road,

as her arms reach out and clutch his
jacket's black leather skin,

as the sun's heat sits below the stirrups, melts
the blacktop tar, the motorcycle gliding

like a boat in a swamp, and the sun's glare
shines in the eye of the car's driver

from the east, who stops to turn
into a street so ordinary that its concrete lawns

are edged with chain-link fences,
and in his eye's glare a small dark speck appears

in the vitreous of road and sky,
and the motorcycle driver decelerates and shouts

something to her, but the wind scatters
the words as she thinks she should not

have let someone else hoist her feet
off the ground, remembering

when she was six her sister
put her on a rope swing that went so high

she hung there, lamely losing traction
with each twisted arc, and so now recalls

the risk in letting the wind scatter parts of you
through the trees like the sun's diamonds.

Untying

My Mother's Hunger

After dark she would sneak into the neighbor's garden
        pulling the string on the overhead closet light

stomach aching feet swollen
        there were shoes of every color and material

looking at the stars she wondered how she had become
        dark leather pumps some

so small the world with each sunrise
        in shades of pink and yellow silk or linen

was a dread she tasted like salt she felt for the
        boxed and shelved nylon stockings in plastic

sweet tomatoes her fingers searching down
        bags shades of taupe and cream or gray

the vine the round and fleshy globes lifting each one
        sequined dresses in black and crusty blue and

juice mixing with her tears spilling
        billowy chiffon in the closet's warm air.

Guide to Meal Planning

Better Homes and Garden Cookbook, 1960

"You won't have to force your family to eat if you set out a breakfast that smells, looks, and tastes good. Try to serve each member of your family the foods he particularly likes. If you take advantage of all the quick-to-fix foods and electric appliances now available, you'll serve a breakfast which meets all of the requirements. What you serve for the noon meal depends on how many members of your family eat at home. If you feed the family at home, plan to serve at least one hot dish. Plan each dinner with as much thought and care as a company meal. Start off with the main dish. Take your pick of potatoes, vegetable, salad and dessert as noted. Add tumblers of milk for the children and milk or coffee for the adults. You will have a meal that is full of health, pretty on the plate, and wonderful to eat. Try to plan your meals for at least a week at a time. In this way, you'll avoid monotony and duplication."

Transaction

Tired of all who come with words, words but no language
I went to the snow covered island. —Tomas Transtromer

My Unitarian Minister was a counselor in transactional analysis
    where people give and take, talk and listen

in predetermined scripts—*I'm only trying to help,* or *I'm OK you're OK,*
    each human interaction reduced to

its smallest and mean-spirited essence. So when I had dinner at his house
    I wasn't surprised that he frowned at his small

and stately wife for the coffee being cold or that
    he was rumored to be having an affair

with a blonde parishioner as in *I deserve it don't I?* He consoled
    me once on my rose chintz couch, touched

my hand meaningfully, handed me a card he had inscribed,
    the blue calligraphy some prophet's words:

what greater thing is there for two human souls than to feel
    that they are joined together? The words were linked

like small blue train cars, silent, unmoving on their tracks.
    That's the trouble with scripts, words chained to one another.

When I heard the sirens one Saturday morning it was them being carried
    away, one dead the other lingering.

When she opened the door to his office and pointed the gun
    was she tired of the words that had no language?

So there was the metal's click, the detonation, his startled face, her hand
    turning to point the gun at herself and the snow

churning as though a wild struggle had occurred and left behind
    like fans in snow the imprint

of wings and feathers, drops of blood and then a lifting off
as though love had been set loose.

Queen Anne's Lace

She bent over the dry ditch
wondering at the lace flowers.
That the world might hold
such a design. Delicacy
in the midst of loss. Not for her
the recitation of the rosary
of sorrow. All of life was
ahead of us and now I see
that lesson for what it was.
Stop! Look for it.
Find it by the road near
rotting steel mills, rusted cars.
Weave it through you,
these petals of silk,
this snowflake of stars.

Coyote

How does it feel to be always searching
the blue-black horizon for the

slightest movement, starving for the next
best thing? Lonely, in the dark,

is the moon a comfort or do you want
instead, the cold of snowdrift

the un-followable trail? I knew
a man like you once who could only

see at a distance. The slightest speck
on the horizon and his eyes

disappeared in pools of black ice.
One day at my door he turned into

the dark, moving away, fast,
like an arrow seeking its next target.

Portland, June 1991

I am sitting on a makeshift terrace
in Oregon in June.

There are six of us.
Our talk is the conversation of waves,
more movement than meaning.

There is a garden in front of us and this;
the smell of mock-orange blossoms,
petals drifting over us, away
and falling on her skirt, my sister's skirt.

She looks up—
her face is flushed and oily.

Our words fall into the air one by one.
Something important or not is being said.

She drifts, halfway into memory now.

She is turning into petals and warm air.

The Fire's Edge

The Portland taxi wheels crunch on gravel
and I touch her as our reflections bleed down
the wet window glass. I will not see her again.
Sisters, we were born on the fire's edge
in a town of sulfur dust, metal water. At night
we sweated the uphill climb to see
the open hearth's unholy glow on the horizon.
On the old mattress with the sinking center
we talked of our futures and who would love us.
The screen door slaps. I turn, see the window,
her face melting in watercolor light.

Clarence and Anita on the Way to the Seminar

When Clarence got into my car he slid
into the back seat waiting for Anita
to hurry it up. Anita chose the front.
On her face an expression that
every woman knows, a little fear,
a little anger, halfway wanting to please.
Being desired and disrespected
at the same time. A king in his carriage
in the car on the way to the seminar.
I drove and Anita sighed, the two of us
in service to his ambition as we weaved
through D.C. traffic, as he grunted
and rustled the New York Times.

Spinning

Hearing of a friend's son
        who slid
off a black silk rope
        of road
into a gully, perhaps
        braking
for some small animal
        in his headlights
slamming metal,
        velocity
into a downward spin,
        I remember
someone said there are endless
        possibilities
in life, just spin and choose.
        Don't believe it.
Each moment's intentions
        are held
in weak arms.
        Just before
he slid and the air
        turned white
there were two roads out,
        brake and slide
or run the damn thing over.

Lines

I'll always love you.

I told her to stay away.

I just have to check with some people.

I have to go back into the office to sort through some things.

That's just powdered sugar.

What do you mean, I spend a lot of time in the bathroom.

We just had a drink.

I want to go over your thesis with you.

The trouble is I don't know how much.

I never sleep with my patients.

Don't touch me in the night, I might hurt you.

The Blue Trail

Cold air hits my face
      my feet stumble
            on tree roots the sun
is strained through trees
      my chest hurts from cold look
            the jewel weed flower
freezes on the stem
      I try not to think
            of you the pond is
coming up
      look how still the lily pads
            are turning brown
I meet a group of women
      with their dogs
            they say a sick raccoon
lingers on the blue trail
      we toss sticks into
            the water
I worry that
      the water is too cold
            you must have
reminded me of someone

Fathers

Once when we were twelve,
playing cards in my living room,
she whispered, *my father*
comes to me in the night.
She said, *first the footsteps,*
then his hands. She learned
to float above herself, look down
on the bed. And I, my father
having left us, thought this must
be what fathers do. Leave your life
or push you from your body.
Daughters hovering, waiting
for the sheets to be quiet,
or at the window looking
down the street for his walk,
his pale hands reaching out for you.

Shredding Old Love Letters

To the CD "Ray"

Here we go again Dan,
into the blades, thin mouth
never smiling. *Afraid and shy,*
why, can't, love you, now
in long thin strands mixed
with looking, never.
Sorry seems to be the hardest
word. Sorry that I never knew
what became of all the time.
Sorry that *something deep inside*
died when we said goodbye.
Sorry you were once here
and now you are running through
my fingers like vintage wine, at last
sweet and opaque and unreadable.

Repurposed

Flagging desire to trumped up vision.
In the repurposed mall, rescued from
the oblivion of cracked concrete, weeds,
and blowing plastic, we lounge
in our leather chairs, watch the movie,
drink our dirty martinis. A relevant
scent blows into the air. We are
in the scene, the mountains and the moon,
and the heroine is struggling against
the elements, trying to find herself.
But also here, in the formerly celebrated
mall of everything where shopping died
and became experience. Not having
to find ourselves, we settle back, sip
and breathe the faux mountain air,
satisfied that we are in the 21st century
in America, where reality is fantasy.

The Accident

He said hold on but he slipped,
fell from my hands.
I find him again and again
in the dream, standing
in the back of the room,
leaning against the wall.
I make my way to him
through rows of folding chairs,
each one a small metallic barrier.
I reach him and he will say:
This journey is full of dust.
We fall through our own lives.

Listening

To those reel-to-reel tapes,
Lou Reed, Jimi Hendrix,
and the Messiah, outlier
winding its way toward
*Worthy is the Lamb who
was slain.* I would find you
again then, body re-gathering
its cells, standing in the dark,
soft eyes, long brown hair.
This winter in a church
filled with light, the words
returned in a chorus,
glistening violins and voices.
Long years ago I listened
for one last configuration
in the plastic spinning tapes.
*He shall stand at the latter day
upon the earth.* Night after night
the curtains lifting in a breeze,
the moon and *forever and ever.
Amen.*

Untying

The motorcyclist, wooly blond
soft skin, left me in a midnight
phone call, breathing silence.
The painter of orange abstracts
pausing in mid-sentence, moved
to the coast of Nova Scotia
where he sent for me in letters.
There were others. Some right
at the wrong time. Some wrong
for all time. I carry their voices
in my ear, their whispers borne
like the dead. Small knots
in the brain. I untie them.

Pay Dirt

On my street of oaks and elms,
duplexes are gone to boarded and
secret insides, to copper strippers,
mantel busters. Streets now canyons
where rivers run in a thin brown milk.
My house with its yellow pillars,
a sunroom where my grandmother
tended her African violets. Small petals
blooming in every season, even
in this city in Ohio where the sky
was a leaden haze, where the soot
was called "pay dirt."

Lost

I am lost in the woods following a dead end trail,
my ability to bushwhack up the steep hill in front of me
in doubt. Sit down, ponder the lost path. I sit in a patch
of moss and think. This wandering. Getting old. Mr. Kinney
lived to be 90. Did his work. Then said, "I'm all used up,"
and died. And what about the sky? Look up. Voyager,
star ship wandering in space for 35 years doing its own work.
Photographing the rings of Saturn, the moons of Jupiter.
Voyager has just entered the heliosphere, a space
where there is no reach of sun, no solar wind, only remnants
of stars millions of year old. Into the quiet zone of no wind.
Work done, battery depleted, no return. This is where all journeys
will end, in a place of windless spirit particles. The sun hits
the spruces, red pines. Breath coming back, body heat down
from cool moss. I get up. Retrace the steps on the trails
marked Slough, Circumferential Dell. Find the intersection
where I went wrong. Where I chose the dead end path.
There it is. Hidden in green. Fern Walk, the path I came in on.

Clean

Her fingers bent in strange ways,
twigs blown in a strong wind.
At night I would stand beside her
at the kitchen sink, dry each dish.
She worried each small bit of grease,
each baked-on remnant of food,
scrubbing as the hot water poured
over her twisted fingers. Balm of heat
on skin, sacrament of cleanliness.

Cake in His Head

Sitting in the stage light,
the strings of the guitar
moving with his fingers,
brown hair falling
over his handsome left eye,
he seemed the perfect cake.
But inside an ingredient
was missing and the batter
had collapsed. He couldn't
be extracted from the pan
except in pieces. Each misshapen
piece a puzzle on the plate.

Enigma Variations

She strained to find the hidden theme,
enigmatic ribbons winding over
and around inventions simple
as a nursery rhyme. She too had outrun
reflection, worshipped at the altar
of false starts. Allegro, presto, andante,
eyes closed, she listened as the music moved
through its own life.

Say

The slant light of winter
through tall windows
where music plays.
We make bird-houses,
read stories, eat fruit.
Their small eyes stare up
into my safe face, not a face
attached to smacking hands.
Hands that would make you want
to take your clothes off,
rub grease in your hair,
jump out the window.
I sit across from each child,
say, *look at me—this is a red apple,*
say *apple,* say *water,*
this is water. Say,
I will remember you.

Small Ceremonies

In the small church beside the river
the speakers search for death's explanation
beyond the casket and the grave.

The music is relieved to be over.

The people go forward no wiser
for these small ceremonies.

Memory, like a faded dress in the closet,
brushes against them now and then—
reminder of how their skin felt to be dressed
and ready for the party.

Later

In the vineyard garden
of green moss, slender trees,
and the bamboo fountain's "shush,"
the six of us talk of you
as you would have been
in this moment.
But the wine glasses clink
and a voice sulks in the distance.
So instead of seeing you
in your son's blue eyes,
we pause and my eyes stray
to the small white butterfly
whose wings are caught
in netted grass.

Under the Trellis

waves of light
  at the edge of the universe
    transport faces
      and time
        enemy of re-visitation
          rains on the window melting down glass
            Mother's lips moving words
              waiting for tires on gravel
                sister's blonde head in the window
                  playing under the trellis
                sister's blonde head in the window
              waiting for tires on gravel
            Mother's lips moving words
          rain on the window melting down glass
        enemy of re-visitation
      and time
    transport faces
  to the edge of the universe
on waves of light

Water

The small disaster
that upended her brain
left a waterfall of thirst,
an unquenchable desire
for drinks, baths, creeks.
We hid the liquids.
Water—the soothing touch,
cradle rocking, soft hand, lullaby,
Tura Lura Lura, siren's song
of hush now don't you cry.
When I last saw her
she brought her small hands
to her mouth and made the sign
 "water, " please water,
run over and through me,
return to me what is lost.

River

A man I knew once told me
that we are small leaves
flowing downstream in a river
of space and time, our destination
love—perhaps unreachable.
But now I see that the river is love
and we are the words
and the words are stones
pushed by the flow, moving,
wedged, or sinking in the silt.

In the Cardiologist's Office

A Whiter Shade of Pale comes on a sort of 70's musak version and memory that
      unwelcomed guest visiting and staying around too long wants

to keep talking and I am waiting for an echocardiogram a sonar picture
      of my heart the thickness of the walls the synchrony of valves the slushing

of the beats and I am back there the night before the accident by a lake and I see the
      moon hear the soft slap of water and the song *her face at first just*

ghostly turned a whiter shade of pale and in the dark see his white teeth
      his long brown hair and feel how uneasily he rides risk's edge

and the next day the car hits us on the Norton and he dies in
      the road and what I can say about it is I keep his orange plaid shirt

for thirty-nine years and his prayer beads from Korea and the song
      when I hear it and at first it is the pain the clenched neck muscles

where I fell against him then the dizziness *the room was humming harder*
      as the ceiling flew away and then just the dark weight of him

my hands circling his chest turning *cartwheels on the floor* my head
      against his back bracing at the place where the car crushed his heart.

Mayflies

On the downhill slope
they circle round

like the black flies of May,
bodies too small to swat.

Wind whisks them away
and then they circle back

to prick with their
anesthetic bite.

Mother in sepia, brown
color of sadness. Father

at the piano scaring the keys
and you holding onto me.

For years we slept
on the old mattress

waking to the mill whistle
and the sulfurous dawn.

Our intentions grew together.
You went first and I said

I'm coming. You slid over,
my steps are slower.

Now moss, now slate, now stone.
Still the flies circling, doubling back.

Notes

Epigraphs_   *Kent State 1970* in the poem *Randomness* refers to the shooting of Sandra Scheuer who was shot wearing a red blouse on May 4, 1970 at Kent State; "The voting machines of Ohio" from *Patience* refers to the breakdown of the voting machines during the 2004 Ohio Presidential election; "That is what space is for," from *Returning to Kent State,* is from page 18 of Gaston Bachelard's, *The Poetics of Space*; the epigraph for *Undercover Dates* concerns the federal undercover operation on the campus after the shootings; *Fear's* epigraph concerns the setting of the concert in October after the shootings; Notes of the students' lawyers in *An Everyday Thing,* refers to found notes from the civil trial; "The secret of this journey is to let the wind," *in The Accident,* is from lines 31 and 32 of *The Journey* by James Wright.

Lyrics_   "tear down the walls" is from *We Can All Be Together* by Paul Kantner, Jefferson Airplane in Fear; lyrics from *Layla* in *Returning to Kent State,* are by Eric Clapton; lyrics in *On the Street Where You Live* are by Nat King Cole from the song of the same name; In *Listening,* "Worthy is the Lamb" and "He shall stand" are from the libretto of the *Messiah* by Handel, lyrics by Charles Jennens; In *Shredding* there are phrases from lyrics on the CD Ray; lyrics in *In the Cardiologist's Office* are from *A Whiter Shade of Pale* by Procol Harum;

The phrase, "small knots in the brain" in *Untying* is derived from the poem, *Having the Having,* line 1, "I tie knots in the strings of my spirit." From Jack Gilbert, *The Collected Works.*

Nancy Richardson's poems have appeared in journals and anthologies and her first chapbook, *Unwelcomed Guest* was published in 2013. In her second chapbook, *The Fire's Edge* (2017), she writes of the events that occurred in the rust-belt of Ohio from the late 1970's onward. *An EveryDay Thing* captures the same period and extends to reflections and memories of the people and events emanating from that time. Nancy lives and works in Vermont. She has worked on educational policy at the federal, state, and local levels in Washington D.C., Massachusetts, and Vermont. She holds a Master's Degree in Fine Arts in Writing from Vermont College of Fine Arts and has served on the Board of the Frost Place in Franconia, New Hampshire.

CPSIA information can be obtained
at www.ICGtesting.com
Printed in the USA
BVHW03s2030270718
522792BV00002B/73/P